MW01282562

Joyful Dancing

*A personal testimony of God's amazing
kindness & compassion*

by

Carol Smullens

authorHOUSE®

AuthorHouse™
1663 Liberty Drive, Suite 200
Bloomington, IN 47403
www.authorhouse.com
Phone: 1-800-839-8640

© 2007 Carol Smullens. All rights reserved.

No part of this book may be reproduced, stored in a retrieval system, or transmitted by any means without the written permission of the author.

First published by AuthorHouse 9/20/2007

ISBN: 978-1-4343-3717-7 (sc)

Cover photo by Nicole Vinisky.

Printed in the United States of America
Bloomington, Indiana

This book is printed on acid-free paper.

*This book is dedicated to the Author
And Perfecter of my faith,
My Lord and Savior, Jesus Christ,
The One who gave me this story to tell.*

Author's Note

This is not my autobiography. This is the story of God's goodness and kindness in the life of an ordinary person. It is the story of my awakening to His presence in my life. Many of the people nearest and dearest to me are not even mentioned, because they did not directly tie in to the particular story that God has me relating here.

I want to thank my friends and family who regularly support and encourage me. My life is so much richer for their presence in my life.

Give thanks to the Lord,
Call on His name;
Make known among the nations
what He has done.
Sing to Him, sing praise to Him;
Tell of all His wonderful acts.
Glory in His holy name;
Let the hearts of those
who seek the Lord rejoice.

Psalm 105:1-4

Preface

I had everything I ever wanted. My husband of over thirty years still treated me like I was his girlfriend. Our grown sons were healthy, intelligent and they still liked us. I had a job I loved. We had enough money to do the things we wanted to do. We traveled wherever we wanted. We owned every conceivable "toy" on the market. We loved each other and we had fun. I thought it couldn't get any better...

But just when you think you've got it "made in the shade", Life comes along and hits you with a body blow that knocks you off your feet.

That's what happened to me. I didn't see it coming, but I know now that I was merrily making my way toward a cliff I didn't know was there. Rather than destroying me, that body blow saved my life.

"For it is by grace you have been saved, through faith—and this not from yourselves, it is the gift of God— not by works, so that no one can boast."

Ephesians 2:8-9

Patrick

I married my college sweetheart one month after graduation. You know how, in the first six months of marriage, there is the thrill of beginning a new life with another person? You just don't get tired of being with each other. It colors everything you do. It makes everything exciting. That's how Patrick and I were for 32 years. Of course, we knew each other better and trusted each other more than newlyweds do, but we still loved being together and doing things together. People used to think that we were a second marriage, because they said we just couldn't be that crazy about each other after more than 30 years. We realized that our marriage was special and we appreciated that fact every day. We knew it was a gift.

We had a dream retirement planned for when Patrick turned 55: we were going to live on a 40 ft catamaran in the Caribbean. We devised a 2-year plan in which we would accomplish this. You have to understand, Pat and I were planners. We thrived on planning. We had jam-packed vacations because of this. Our family motto was "Work hard. Play hard." Step 1 of this two-year plan was to learn all we could about living aboard a boat – everything from diesel repair to the ins and outs of getting your mail when you don't have a permanent address to clever ways of doing without all the things we had spent a lifetime accumulating. We had fun traveling to boat shows and boat builders all over the east coast, in places like Nova Scotia, Mississippi, Annapolis, and Miami. We probably went aboard and checked out more than 500 boats over the two years, looking for the perfect fit for our new life.

Step 2 was to sell almost everything we owned – property and possessions – our house, apartment buildings, cars, motorcycles, numerous bicycles, small boats, clothes, books, furniture and several billion knickknacks. This involved mind-numbing decisions about what to sell by auction or e-Bay or collector, what to give away, what to store for future generations (family heirlooms and precious memorabilia) and what to just plain throw away. The goal was to get it down to a few boxes. The last step was to shop for a boat that would be seaworthy, comfortable and fairly easy for relative novices to handle. While we had been sailing for years, it had been primarily on large lakes. We were now contemplating something far more challenging.

The plan was that, a few months before departure, Pat would retire and finish up the liquidation process. Once everything was sold, we would move into a small apartment while Pat outfitted the boat and I continued to work. When he was done, I would retire and we would sail off into the sunset. Sounded good to us. It kept us going through the exhausting task we had taken on. When things got stressful, we would encourage each other with, "Next year we'll be sitting on the deck of our boat gazing at Paradise. This will all be a distant memory". It was a beautiful dream. The problem, of course, is that Life doesn't always turn out the way you plan. The day after we moved into the temporary apartment, we found out that Pat had stage IV pancreatic cancer.

This was unthinkable. I was the one who had multiple sclerosis. I was the one who'd had brain surgery. I was the one who had health issues. Not Pat. He'd never had anything more serious than the flu. The last time he was in the hospital was when he was born in 1947. He ran every day. He was careful with what he ate. He always got enough sleep. He didn't drink, smoke or use drugs. How could Pat suddenly have a serious illness? It just did not compute. We did all the research we could. We wrote doctors and hospitals all over the world. I still remember arguing and pleading with a doctor in the Philippines. As it turned out, the normal course of chemotherapy was all we could come up with and they didn't have much confidence in that. The doctors told us from the first day that Pat wasn't likely to survive this. I refused to believe Pat would die. I'd been in love with this man since I was 18 years old. I'd built my whole world around him. I just couldn't lose him. It was not going to happen. I wouldn't let it.

After a few months of chemotherapy, the cancer had spread even further. We scanned the Internet daily for any clinical trials that would let him in. We had everyone we knew praying rosaries and novenas. We were Catholic and that's all we knew to do. There was one doctor we found in NYC who had an alternative program that had published some very promising results with pancreatic cancer. I knew that this was it! This was our "miracle". We faxed a huge stack of test results and reports from his doctors and applied for the program. I was excited. I knew this was our answer. It had to be.

Pat was still in remarkably good condition, considering his illness. Why wouldn't the doctor want him in his trial? The next day I received a fax at work telling me that the doctor was very sorry, but there was no hope, that nothing could help my husband now. I was absolutely stunned. My knees actually buckled. I realized for the first time that Pat was going to die. You have to understand that I wasn't just saying I believed he would be cured while deep down inside I was afraid he was going to die. I truly believed he'd be cured. I thought we would have a big scare and then be extremely grateful for his recovery. I never once thought it was a losing battle. That's why I was so stunned. I don't think I even cried. I was just numb.

The next morning was Saturday, January 10, 2004. It was a cold winter morning in upstate New York. I was soaking in the bathtub, completely devastated. My world had just been shattered. Everything I had planned and hoped and dreamed was about to come crashing down. I was in despair. I never really knew what that word meant before. This was cold, empty, totally devoid of hope. I had nothing ahead of me. Everything that I counted on for security and even identity in my life was being taken from me. It was unbearable. I was lost.

Then – suddenly - the most amazing thing happened: I felt almost as if someone had put an arm around me. I didn't feel a physical touch, but I felt the same comfort I would've felt, had someone put an arm around me. It's hard to explain, but I remember it so clearly. It startled me. I was instantly and overwhelmingly filled with such joy that I couldn't contain it! I went from complete emptiness to overflowing joy in the blink of an eye. And I knew some things that I hadn't known before. I hadn't heard any voices. I just knew. I jumped up, threw a towel around me and ran to Pat. I stood there, dripping all over the bedroom floor as I told him that I had just met God, in the bathtub! That He had told me that everything was going to be all right. He loved us and was going to take care of us.

He also told me that we had been going about things all wrong. We had not prayed from our hearts; we said memorized prayers. We had not read His Word. We had been giving God one hour a week in church and then ignoring Him the rest of the time. We had not asked the Creator of the Universe what He wanted from us. We had been just doing things our own way. Rather than being upset that God had told me that we had been wrong, I was excited. Almighty God actually took the time to personally correct us. I found tremendous joy in that. By this time I was talking a mile a minute. I said "We have to pray from our hearts - every day - for God's guidance. We have to ask Him what He wants us to do. We need to read the Bible. We need to learn what it says and how we are to live our lives", and on and on.

Eventually I began coming back down to earth and, knowing that Pat was a cautious and skeptical person by nature, I realized that there was a very good chance he was going to think that the strain of the last few months had finally gotten to me. I was afraid to make eye contact. I was so afraid he would be skeptical about what I told him. I couldn't handle that. I could take it about almost anything else, but not about this. This was too important and I knew it was the truth. I finally looked up at him and he said the most unexpected thing. He said, "That's what I want, too." That was the most precious moment of my life. It was completely out of character for Pat to agree with something so unusual so quickly. Only God could have made that happen.

We immediately got down on our knees and prayed. If you have ever seen a couple of Catholics who have never prayed from their hearts out loud before, then you know it was pretty awkward. We didn't have a clue what to say. We said something like, "Dear God, We love you. We praise you. Please help us." We were like a pair of kindergarteners. OK, back to the Internet. Google "How to pray". It said we should pray for our enemies. Pat and I didn't really have any enemies so we settled for praying for some people we didn't like that much. We began each day praying for guidance and ended each day thanking God for getting us through the day.

We were praying for Pat to be healed, but little by little the Holy Spirit changed our prayers so that we were praying for the strength to face what each of us had to face. For Pat, that was death. For me, it was life without Pat. We only had three more weeks together, but it was very special. Pat had a peaceful death and I was the strongest person at the funeral. Many people were afraid to come to the funeral, because the thought of seeing me with Pat gone was too much to bear. They assumed that I would be inconsolable. They did not know that I had found the only true comfort there is: Jesus Christ. I was the one doing the consoling, rather than the one being consoled.

"...that the God of our Lord Jesus Christ, the Father of glory, may give to you the spirit of wisdom and revelation in the knowledge of Him"

Ephesians 1:17

A New Perspective

During this time, I read the Bible as best as I could on my own. The Psalms were very comforting. Even though I had no background knowledge of Israel's history, I was moved by the messages of love contained there. Since I was serious about wanting to learn the Bible, I bought a book that was a companion study guide. I was reading the introduction and every time it made a scripture reference, I would look it up. Being such a novice, I didn't realize that there was both a book of John as well as 1 John. So when it directed me to John 20:31, I turned to 1 John and was confused. It only had 5 chapters. Why was it sending me to chapter 20? I turned the pages and flipped back and forth like an idiot for a few minutes, totally confounded, wondering what it was I had missed. In the flipping of pages, one passage kept catching my eye so I decided to read it. It was 1 John, chapter 3, verses 18-20 (in the New Living Translation):

"Dear children, let's not merely say that we love each other; let us show the truth by our actions. Our actions will show that we belong to the truth, so we will be confident when we stand before God. Even if we feel guilty, God is greater than our feelings, and he knows everything."

I was a brand new believer, less than 3 weeks old. I knew nothing about the Bible. I knew very little about God but I knew – absolutely,

7

positively for sure knew – that this verse was written to tell me to forgive myself about my mother. I read it and felt a jump in my heart. I burst out crying in such tender gratitude for the removal of this secret burden.

I took care of my mother for the last few years of her life. She lived in an upstairs apartment in my home and I prepared her meals and took her to the doctor and generally oversaw all her needs. I was kind to her and never let her know that sometimes in my heart I grumbled about having to be upstairs tending to her when I wanted to be downstairs spending time with my husband and kids. Not all the time, but sometimes.

When she died, it was painful to remember her, because I felt guilty. I should have loved her more. I should have been more selfless. I should have realized it was a privilege to care for my mother. I shoved it in the back of my mind and tried not to think about it. Then I read this verse. It told me very strongly that I had done all that God had expected of me and that He knew my heart better than I did. What a release! He healed me of something I'd forgotten I suffered from. What amazing tenderness! God is not into guilt. He is about correction, but not shame. That comes from a different source.

It was also at this time I learned that even a brand new believer has all the discernment available to him through the Holy Spirit that dwells within us from the moment we are saved. I turned on the TV to the religious channel and saw a televangelist speaking. He presented himself as someone engaged in the work of Jesus but his behavior suggested otherwise. He was saying that he was not willing to wait until heaven for his rewards –he wanted them right now. Every word he spoke revealed his self-serving motivation. Even though millions of people appear to revere this man, I knew that he was not of God. I knew that he was out for himself. I didn't need years of Bible study to realize that fact. There have been a few times over the last couple of years that I have talked to someone who claims to be a Christian and something in my spirit tells me to beware. The Bible tells us that there will always be people who will masquerade as Christians in order to take advantage of people whose guards are down. Where better to find people who are vulnerable than in church?

I had been advised that widows often make mistakes by acting too rashly, so I determined to take my time and see what happened. About a week after the funeral, I went back to work. I had always loved my job and all my friends were there. It would be better than sitting around my empty apartment dwelling on my loss. Everyone was very kind to me and supportive, but the trouble was, I had lost all enthusiasm for my job. I would sit in a meeting about strategy for a new project and I simply didn't care anymore. I just wanted to study the Bible. I had such a hunger to learn. I knew there was so much I'd been missing. I had a lot of catching up to do.

At night I would go home and start "trolling": I would search the Internet for any Bible studies or prayer groups at area churches. Once a week was not nearly often enough for me. I needed more. I began going to Loudonville Community Church, an evangelical church that a friend attended, and found it was such a breath of fresh air. For the first time ever I was attending a service where they taught God's word – all of it, not just the selected parts they were comfortable with. I was no longer just a spectator. I was engaged. I was interested. I attended adult Sunday school and took classes to prepare for my immersion baptism.

I believe that God protects His baby Christians with a Father's loving tenderness. I know I was naïve and could've wound up entangled in some cult or worse, but God didn't let that happen. He even protected me when I was "trolling". (By the way, I do <u>not</u> recommend that a woman go to a strange church at night alone! That was a foolish and dangerous thing to do. At one of the places I went to, the people scared the life out of me. They actually told me they weren't going to let me leave until I spoke in tongues! I thank God for His protection that night.) I saw an ad for a church service on a Thursday night at some church a few miles away. It was in an area I was not familiar with.

So there I was, all alone, driving on a dark stretch of road, looking at the street numbers with difficulty. When I looked forward, I saw that the car in front of me had stopped suddenly and was about a half car length in front of me. I cannot think that fast, but before I knew what happened, my car was turned to the left, pulled into a driveway that had a chain across it with just space for one car to fit and stopped. I had no idea what had happened. I didn't consciously turn the car, but it got turned. I was never one to believe in supernatural intervention, but I believe to this day that an angel turned the steering wheel. It happened far too quickly and, if I were to react, I would have turned to the right, because I couldn't see around the car ahead of me to see if there was oncoming traffic in the lane. Also, I did not see the little short driveway until I was in it. It was very dark, no streetlights, and no houses or other buildings on that side of the street. I had no way of knowing it was there.

About a month after Pat died, I began to worry that maybe he wasn't actually saved after all. I mean, he did pray with me and he said he wanted to turn to God and seek His will, but toward the end when he was so weak and tired, I did almost all the talking and praying out loud. I didn't actually hear him say the words to invite Jesus into his heart. It began to build up until I really obsessed about it. I prayed to God that He would somehow get a message to me that Pat was saved. I didn't know what form this would take, but I believed He could and would do it somehow.

Now here's where it gets silly. I started expecting a message over the radio or TV or on some billboard. That somehow someone would say something only I knew was a message meant for me. I didn't have any idea how the God of the universe would communicate to me. I now know He can use anything or anyone. About two weeks after I began praying for this, often tearfully and desperately, I took a day off from work to spend with my friend, Rowena. She and her husband, Dennis, were the only believers I knew back then. We had been friends for about 20 years and we spent a fun day discussing Scripture and looking stuff up in the Bible. I didn't know much, but I was eager to learn. Later Dennis came home from work and the three of us carried on an animated dinner conversation. I learned so much from this wonderful couple who had been believers far longer than I had.

As I was getting ready for my long drive home, I told them about my concerns that Pat might not have been actually saved. Dennis said something along the lines of "He didn't have to say the exact words…if he agreed with you in prayer in his heart…" and I knew. That was my answer. I felt a strong confirmation in my spirit that he was speaking the truth. I have never worried about it since. I know with all my heart that my husband is with the Lord and I will one day see him again.

The LORD had said to Abram, "Leave your country, your people and your father's household and go to the land I will show you."

A New Start

Eventually I started to get a strong impression that I should retire and move out to Santa Barbara, CA, where our oldest son, Michael lived. It seemed that everywhere I looked, Santa Barbara came up. If I picked up a book to read, it was written by an author from Santa Barbara. I met a new couple at church and, of course, they had just moved there from Santa Barbara. I turned on the TV (in Albany, NY) and the announcer said "Today in Santa Barbara...." These three things happened in a 24 hour period. I had no idea if that was God urging me to move there, but it sure felt like it, so I gave my notice at work for right after my scheduled baptism at Loudonville Community Church.

I planned to move out there at the end of May, so I flew out with my sister-in-law, Bonnie, in April to find a church and an apartment. I was such a beginner at praying for God's provision, but I told Him I needed an apartment, preferably in the Harbor area where Pat and I used to stay when we visited Michael, because it was near the bike paths that run along the beach. Because I have MS, I cannot walk for very long, but I can bike for hours. I also asked if I could possibly get a two-bedroom so I would have someplace for our other son, David, to stay when he came home from college, but if the expense of a two-bedroom was too much, we could make do with a one-bedroom.

My budget was very tight. I would have to live on a reduced pension, because I retired before age 55. Choosing to live in one of the most expensive cities doesn't seem to be a wise financial move, does it? I figured

I could not afford more than $1400 per month, which was about double the rent back in upstate NY. So I prayed this and deliberately did <u>not</u> look at the classifieds for an apartment until two days before Bonnie and I flew out there. Then I made a lot of phone calls. Many of the apartments were in the wrong location. Some cost too much. Others were already rented. I left my number on a few answering machines. The night before we left, I got one return call. Only one. It was from a landlord who had a two-bedroom apartment in the Harbor area, two blocks from the beach and bike paths and, oh, yes, the rent was $1400. I was so excited at how precisely God had answered my prayer. I felt He was taking care of me. Although in the past I had always felt the need to plan things out way in advance, I had no fear of going along with Him leading me step by step.

The landlord, Alberto, was very nice on the phone and said he would not even advertise the apartment until I had seen it. When we got to Santa Barbara, we looked at the apartment and it was just what I asked for: no frills, but clean, safe and convenient.

I also had to find a church. This was new to me. When you are a Catholic, you just go to the closest Catholic church. Now it was different, I had to put some critical thought into the process. Back to the Internet. I searched for evangelical churches in the city. After awhile, I had it narrowed down to three contenders. When I got to Santa Barbara, I set up interviews with the pastors at those churches. Each church sounded good. I was a bit confused when I got to Calvary Chapel, though. I was looking for stained glass windows or, at the very least, a steeple with a cross. What I found was a warehouse in an industrial park. I called the church on my cell phone and confirmed that this was indeed where the church was. Once I was inside, though, it was so comfortable and inviting that I was immediately put at ease. That Sunday I went to services in each church, but when I got to Calvary, I knew I was home. The tears started flowing as soon as the worship music began. We flew home, I got baptized, packed up my few belongings and drove across country to Santa Barbara to begin a whole new life.

My trip out west was a very healing time. I listened to Christian teachers like Charles Stanley and David Jeremiah as well as Christian music. I learned and I worshiped and I cried for the 11 days that I was in the "wilderness". By the time I got to my new home, I was ready to live a life that was completely different than anything I had ever experienced. My focus had been irrevocably changed. My life was no longer going to be about how much pleasure I could cram into it. It was going to be about seeking God in every area of my life. I had so much to learn, but God had cleared the decks. I was ready.

"Show me your ways, O LORD, teach me your paths;
guide me in your truth and teach me, for you are God my Savior,
and my hope is in you all day long."

Psalm 25:4-5

I arrived in Santa Barbara on a Friday and that Sunday I went to the 8:00 am service at Calvary Chapel. Before I went in, I took a moment in my car and said, "Here I am, Lord, reporting for duty. Whatever you ask of me, the answer is 'Yes!'". When I got inside, the pastor said , "We need 20 volunteers to take on a Jesus Assignment. You have to give your answer before you know what it is. Anyone interested?" I was the very first person on the stage. If you knew me, you'd know that this is not something I was inclined to do. In fact, it was something that I usually avoided like the plague, but I meant it when I said I'd do anything God asked of me.

So I took the challenge and that summer I learned a lot about praying for and then waiting on an answer from God. It truly was a challenge, since this was uncharted territory for me. I'd had no role models. I'd always been taught to be independent and to accomplish things through my own effort and strength. Now all the rules had changed and I didn't know what they were. But God is so good. He had gifted me with such a trust of Him that, when I didn't know what to do, I just told Him that. God and I had some wonderful talks that summer and He gently and lovingly guided me to where He wanted me to be.

When God saved me, He wiped the slate clean. I didn't carry over a lot of debris from my former religion. So I started from scratch. I felt strongly that I was not to get another job. I was to learn about God. I signed up for every Bible study that was not specifically for men or children. For the first year, I had eight studies going each week plus Sunday and Wednesday church services and two prayer groups. It was really beautiful the way God orchestrated this. Each of my studies was different in their focus. Some were historical, some were about God's nature, some were about prophecy. Some were about how we are to live in light of who God is. I learned so much about God's character and His great love for us.

I had spent 54 years going to church every week and I did not learn any of these things I was now learning. It was thrilling. The added bonus to all these studies was that I got to know a lot of people in a very short time. After about 3 months, people thought I had been there years and years. When I would refer to having moved there 3 months prior, they would be shocked. This was God's way of creating a whole new life for me and getting me up to speed fast.

I can only speak of my own and my family's experience as Catholics. Since everyone in my family had always been Catholic, I never really gave serious thought to checking out any other way. It had been drummed into my head that the Roman Catholic Church was the "one true church". It was actually considered a sin to even attend a wedding in a Protestant church when I was very young. Since I had been so indoctrinated in this religion, I never questioned it. This never ceases to astound me today, that I would so unquestioningly follow whatever I was taught. In the rest of my life, I was a researcher. I always checked things out and analyzed them – purchases, vacations, jobs, medical treatments - but not the most important issue of my life.

Looking back I know there were some things that kind of bothered me, but I never actually put them into words. I always wondered if God was more impressed by 100 Hail Marys than He was by 20 Hail Marys. I mean, when you repeat a prayer that you have memorized like that, over and over, you can actually be thinking of something else while you do it, like a grocery list or what you're going to do later in the day. The heart isn't usually engaged. Isaiah 29:13 says:

"These people come near to me with their mouth and honor me with their lips, but their hearts are far from me. Their worship of me is made up only of rules taught by men."

It saddens me to admit it but that describes me back then. I also had a problem with saying prayers and obtaining indulgences for the souls in Purgatory. If God was perfectly fair, how could He commute their sentences based on what we, the living, did? What about those who didn't have any friends or family to pray for them? It didn't seem right to me. The biggest problem I now have with my previous religious education is that we were never encouraged to read the Bible. I missed out on so much because of that. I didn't know my Father or my Savior. I had imperfect and incomplete snippets of who they were, but I could've had it straight from the Source.

Nowhere in the Bible is there any mention that we should worship Mary. It is true that she was a godly woman who humbly obeyed God and was the human mother of our Savior, Jesus Christ, but the Catholic church teaches that she was born sinless. That doesn't line up with what the Bible teaches. Romans 3:10 says:

"There is no one righteous, not even one"

and Romans 3:23-24 says:

"for all have sinned and fall short of the glory of God, and are justified freely by his grace through the redemption that came by Christ Jesus."

All have sinned. That includes Mary. In the Gospel of Luke, Mary refers to her Savior. A sinless person does not need a savior. The Catholic church has elevated Mary to a level of co-redemptrix with her Son. They teach that we must go through Mary and have her intercede for us to her Son. 1 Timothy 2:5 says:

"For there is one God and one Mediator between God and men, the Man Christ Jesus".

If Mary was what the Church has claimed she is, why don't any of the books in the New Testament even hint at this?

Thankfully God has opened my eyes and changed my heart. He has so lovingly arranged for me to learn about Him. One of the things I love most about God is that He doesn't want us to be consumed by guilt or anxiety. He wants us to let Him guide us into perfect peace. Isaiah 26:3 says:

"You will keep in perfect peace him whose mind is steadfast because he trusts in you."

He isn't a harsh God who wants to see us squirm. He is a loving Father who wants to give us everything that is for our good. Not necessarily everything we want, but everything we need. All we really need is Him.

"For we are God's workmanship, created in Christ Jesus to do good works, which God prepared in advance for us to do."

Ephesians 2:10

"For we are God's workmanship, created in Christ Jesus to do good works, which God prepared in advance for us to do."

Ephesians 2:10

Ministry & Missions

When I knew I would be moving out to Santa Barbara, I thought I would volunteer at the City Rescue Mission. I never had ambitions to be a leader, but I have always been a good follower. I would be the Soup Lady. I figured I would smile and say something kind as I ladled the soup onto the plates of the poor and downtrodden. I figured that God didn't have much use for a computer programmer in His kingdom work, but I could at least be a nice Soup Lady. Funny how God's mind works so differently from mine. He had a very different game plan than I did.

After several months of Bible studies, I really wanted to serve in some way. I love children so I signed up to work in the Children's Ministry. Calvary has an awesome Children's program. I spoke to the person in charge, filled out the forms, got pastor references from back east and even got fingerprinted at the police station. Then I went to serve and, after a couple of months, realized that it wasn't my calling. I didn't know why, but it just wasn't. I really wanted to serve, but I was going about it in the wrong way. I was doing the deciding. I wasn't letting the Lord lead me. Knowing that I didn't mean any disrespect, that I was just new at this, the Lord dealt with me very gently. I said, "Lord, I don't have any particular talents or skills but I am friendly. If you know of anyone who needs a friend, I'm your girl".

A couple nights later, a woman I knew slightly asked me after our prayer group if I wanted to get some coffee. I agreed and, since we couldn't find anything open and I lived close by, we went to my apartment. After a bit of conversation, this beautiful, talented woman who, by all outward appearances, seemed to have it all, broke down crying that she just couldn't make any friends. I knew immediately that God had sent her to me. So I befriended her and we would meet now and then and pray and talk. I thought this was nice. Then He sent me another woman. Then another. Often they needed someone to talk to and I was certainly available. I no longer had a husband or a job or a house. My children were grown. Even my beloved dog, Genny, had died the year before Pat did. I was the most available woman you ever met!

Sometimes the reason they were sent to me was, because I got to know so many people so quickly, that I could plug them in somewhere. Sometimes it was because they had suffered a loss like I had. Whatever the reason, it became apparent that God had decided that I would have a ministry of meeting with women who needed someone to talk to. I would arrange to meet them at the beach or a coffee shop or wherever was convenient.

In the meantime, I went on a mission trip to Ensenada, Mexico. My roommate was a woman named Kim Paden. We hit it off at once and when we returned home continued to be good friends. I started going to 2 groups she told me about: M-PAC (Mothers Praying for Adult Children) and Shekinah Glory.

A couple of months later, a woman at one of my Bible studies, Kim Newton, suggested that I pray about going with her and two others on a mission trip to Romania to work with abandoned and orphaned babies. I told her I would pray about it. I have to admit, I still wasn't sure if I'd know whether I was supposed to go or not. I prayed about it and then decided that I would just assume I was to go unless the Lord closed doors for me. He didn't, so I went. I have since learned that if you pray about a decision and want to know if it is in God's will, you check if 1) it is in alignment with what the Bible teaches (this was – see James 1:27), 2) God opens the doors for it to happen and 3) you have an inner peace about it. God doesn't make it impossible to discern His will. He doesn't set us up for failure. That's not in His nature.

There would be four of us going: Kim, her 13-year-old daughter, Christy, and the leader, Machal (pronounced "Michelle"), who had been there before. We met and prayed every chance we got. Machal gave us invaluable insight into what the people were like and what we could do to be of service to them. Romania was quite an eye-opener for me. I had traveled quite a bit before, but always as a tourist on vacation. This time I was going in order to serve. Our goal was to help out taking care of the babies that R.O.C.K. Ministries has charge over at Victor Gomoiu Hospital. R.O.C.K. (Romania Outreach to Christ's Kids) was founded in order to fill a very desperate need. Because of a failed attempt by former leader, Nicolae Ceauşescu, to build up the strength of the nation by increasing its population dramatically, women were having babies they could not afford to keep. As a result, after giving birth, many women walked out of the hospital and left their babies behind.

The hospital became a default orphanage, but it was not equipped to give the babies the individualized care they needed. Babies began to exhibit signs of detachment. They would not make eye contact. They became sickly. Some died. An amazing woman named Nannette Gonzalez changed all that when she helped found R.O.C.K. She negotiated with the hospital to have a special area where these abandoned babies were kept. She would see to it that they were cared for. Today there is a staff of over 20 people who run the foundation and take care of the babies.

As a regular part of their routine, they have small groups of volunteers, like us, from churches in the US who come for 10 days at a time to help out. The volunteers show up at the hospital first thing in the morning and get the babies up for washing and feeding. I can't express in words how sweet those little babies are. They greeted us with smiles and outstretched arms, just bursting to be picked up and cuddled. A chaotic hour would go by, then when everyone was cleaned and dressed, it was time to sit in the rocking chairs and feed them and play with them until nap time. The R.O.C.K. staff just love those babies. It is evident in everything they do. They are "their" babies.

In the afternoon, we had different activities lined up. One day was a visit to foster families that R.O.C.K. set up. These families are carefully checked out. They must be Christian, sober, non-smokers and have clean, neat, stable homes. R.O.C.K. pays the woman of the family a living wage so she can stay home and take care of her own as well as her foster children. They also supply them with whatever they need for the children in terms of food, clothes and diapers, etc. The families seem to have really bonded with these kids as evidenced by the way the babies interact with them. These children who were unwanted by their birth families have found love and security through Jesus Christ working via R.O.C.K. Ministries. Our God is an awesome God!

Another day, some of us went to see the state run orphanage. It was not a place you'd want the kids to wind up. In fact one of the R.O.C.K. workers grew up in an orphanage and she told us about the stigma attached to someone who was an orphan in Romania. It is not what we would think. In our country, an orphan who works hard and makes something of themselves is to be applauded. Employers are maybe even more kindly disposed to them than kids who have had every advantage. In Romania, it is the opposite. If an employer were to find out that one of his employees was an orphan, they would most likely fire him. This is part of the reason R.O.C.K. goes all out to place their children in good foster families. These families would love to adopt the children, but there are numerous political deterrents.

One of the afternoon activities we really looked forward to was meeting with "Julie's Street Kids". Julie was a tall, thin, soft-spoken Romanian woman who was part of the hospital staff at R.O.C.K. In her off time, she would meet with street kids. Most of these are not actually homeless - they are instead from homes where they are not cared for and are not allowed to go to school. They are, in fact, forced to go out on the streets to get money any way they can. They are not clean and the lice treatment was so popular we wished we had brought five times as much as we had. It was heart-wrenching to see them asking Julie questions about how long to keep it on and how to comb it out.

Julie ran a tight ship. It was very obvious that they loved and respected her. Even though she was firm with them, they could tell she cared about them. That was something they had never experienced before. She led them in worship and taught them the gospel. They knew all the praise songs by heart and sang out at the top of their lungs. This moved us to tears. After the worship and the message, Julie fed them. She used her own meager salary to buy them big sandwiches and snacks. She always had enough to fill them up.

We had prayed beforehand that God would somehow overcome the language barrier. Julie spoke English, but none of the kids did. We were prepared to just be spectators to Julie's ministry, but the kids were so taken by our digital cameras that we had to keep taking their pictures and then showing them. They kept begging and posing. It was so cute. The scarves and hats that the women of our church had knitted for them were a huge hit. We were able to give them to all who needed them.

God really blessed our trip. We learned so much and our friendship grew through our shared experience. We felt our hearts enlarge when we could see God at work in places that were strange to us. It just made it so apparent that He is everywhere and in everything.

"Unless the LORD builds the house, they labor in vain who build it."

Psalm 127:1

Women Of Gilead

On the night before we returned home from Romania, we were just talking and sharing about our hopes and dreams. I told Kim about my developing ministry of meeting with women. She told me about how she and some of her friends had been praying for years for a safe place for women to go to where they could get support when they are facing a trial of some sort. On the 13 hour flight home the next day, the idea for a women's ministry was born. We met in the back of the plane and talked and talked about it with growing excitement. We started meeting weekly at Starbucks to pray over what God would have us do. We also prayed at home. One night in prayer, I said, "Lord, please give us a name so we don't have to keep calling it 'our new ministry'".

Immediately, the word "refuge" came to mind. Then "city of refuge". Then "Gilead was a city of refuge". (Actually that was the only one I knew by name). Then, "Gilead had a healing balm", and finally "we would be the women of Gilead". When I told this to Kim, she loved it. So that's what we named our ministry: Women of Gilead. We continued to cover this idea with prayer. One night in prayer I clearly saw the face of Kim Paden, the woman I met in Mexico. We decided to ask her if she'd like to join us and she did. Months later, it was discovered that she had cancer and had to have weeks of radiation treatments. She said that knowing God had hand-picked her to be a part of this fledgling ministry was a big comfort and encouragement to her during this scary period of her life.

There was a man in our church named Jos, whom I knew from a prayer group at Calvary Chapel. He had the gift of the Word of Knowledge, i.e., sometimes God would give him a specific, prophetic word for someone.

One evening, shortly after we returned from Romania, I told him about our trip and especially about Women of Gilead. As I was speaking, he asked for a paper and pencil. He sketched a house with an off-center roofline and a picket fence. He said the front yard would be a bit neglected and messy, but just needed a little sprucing up. He said it would be in a prime area and have good transportation. The final thing he said was that it would be donated for our use. Since I'd had no previous experience with the Word of Knowledge, I wasn't sure how to take this information, but I knew and trusted Jos, so I just filed this tidbit away in the back of my mind as a happy possibility.

We had come back from Romania in March, prayed and planned through April and May, then in June we decided to do a trial run to see if God would bless this undertaking. We took our own money and sublet an apartment for 2 months. Because it was furnished and "coincidentally" belonged to the Campus Crusade for Christ couple, it was perfect for our purposes. It was attractive, comfortable, and had shelves full of Biblical reference books and scripture everywhere throughout the apartment. We made an announcement at church and told all of our friends. We printed up some business cards on the computer and put my cell phone number on it. Then we waited to see what the Lord would do. He did "exceedingly, abundantly more" than we could ever have imagined!

We went into this ministry with one fundamental premise: we would not be the ones doing the ministering, that would be the job of the Holy Spirit. We were determined to use the Word of God to be the only counsel we relied on. One of the very first women to come there, came reluctantly. Her marriage was dead and had been for some time. She and her husband flew in to Santa Barbara to see relatives to discuss the fact that the marriage was over. One of the relatives was a friend of ours from the men's ministry who picked them up at the airport and dropped the wife off with us while he ministered to the husband.

While we were waiting for her to arrive, Kim and I went through our scripture reference books looking for appropriate scriptures to give her. We started looking up scriptures on divorce, then decided that maybe it shouldn't be about divorce. Maybe it should be about marriage or relationships. No, maybe love. Then we looked up at each other and we both realized at the same time: it shouldn't be about any of those things. It should be about her relationship with Jesus Christ. When she arrived, we prayed and we told her that since we didn't know what her relationship with the Lord was like, since we didn't know what she did or didn't know, we were going to start from scratch. We led her through a time of silent confession, then submission to the Lord. We used "Roman's Road" to explain the gospel to her. (See the last page of this book for a description of "Romans Road").

Afterward, the change in her was so dramatic, we could hardly believe it. She was so excited, she nearly cracked our ribs when she hugged us goodbye! Her husband had also been touched by the Holy Spirit. By the time they left a few days later, they had recommitted themselves to Jesus and to each other. She resigned from her job, which had been a breeding ground for some of their problems, and they planned on taking up a hobby that they both enjoyed, where previously they had done everything separately. Nearly two years later, I am told they are closer than ever.

Those two months were filled with blessing after blessing. Women came to us for prayer for everything from addiction to marital trouble to financial problems to crises of faith. We started each day submitting our will to God and asking Him to speak through us. He was so faithful to give each woman what she needed. Since we were open 3 days a week, we wound up being open a total of only 22 days. During that time we ministered to almost 300 women!

Some came to us. Some we met elsewhere. Some we prayed with over the phone. We went to the hospital to comfort a woman whose husband had died a month before and was now waiting for the doctors to tell her if her son would die of the same disease. We came alongside a woman whose teenage daughter died suddenly and tragically. One day we went to a woman's home who was drinking herself to death. She called us for help, but didn't know what she wanted to do. We brought her to our place, fed her, let her sleep on the couch for awhile, prayed with her when she awoke, made phone calls on her behalf and finally got her into a detox unit. Today she is clean and sober and has a very responsible job. I see her at church regularly and she just radiates joy.

"Therefore I tell you, do not worry about your life, what you will eat or drink; or about your body, what you will wear. Is not life more important than food, and the body more important than clothes? Look at the birds of the air; they do not sow or reap or store away in barns, and yet your heavenly Father feeds them. Are you not much more valuable than they? Who of you by worrying can add a single hour to his life?"

Matthew 6:25-30

It became very clear that God was blessing this ministry. After our sublet period was over, we no longer had a physical place, but we had a cell phone and the faith to believe that God would provide. We continued to meet with women, but now it was at the beach or Starbucks, wherever it was convenient for them. We put the word out that we were looking for a place. We considered renting, but it was going to take some doing to raise the necessary money each month. Our pastor, Ricky Ryan, advised us to wait. He felt that someone would come through with a donated place for us.

Every once in awhile a generous person would offer some space that they had available, but each time we looked at the place, it just didn't feel right. We knew that there were certain factors that limited our search. Privacy was essential. No women would feel safe enough to come to us and unburden herself if she thought she would be seen or overheard. We needed to be in an easy-to-reach location. We wanted to be able to leave our reference books and computer and records there. If we had to share space with others, it just wouldn't work. After turning down place after place, we started to feel that maybe God was providing, but that we were being too picky.

Then came the phone call. I was sitting at my computer at home writing an e-mail when the phone rang. It was a woman who did not go to our church, but had stopped by for prayer when we were in our sublet several months earlier. She asked if we had found a place yet. I said no. She sounded very relieved. She said she felt that God wanted her to donate her rental property for our use. She needed to get a few hundred dollars to cover the taxes, but we could have it for an indefinite period of time and do whatever we wanted to it.

I was still a little distracted by my e-mail, but I asked her where it was. She told me. I then asked her if it had a picket fence. After a very slight pause, she said it did. That got my attention. I arranged to meet her there the next day. It looked exactly like the sketch Jos drew! It had a picket fence. It had the off-center roofline and the front yard desperately needed some clean-up work. There was a bus stop across the street. It fit his description completely.

About a month later, I took our benefactor out to brunch to thank her for what she was doing and we laughed over the odd conversation we'd had on the phone. She couldn't figure out why I asked about a picket fence, rather than how many rooms the house had or whether or not there was a yard. I mean, who cares whether it has a picket fence or not? She was amazed when I shared with her Jos' vision of the house. She requested that she remain anonymous. She felt that God had asked her to donate the use of the house, but not to be involved with the ministry itself. For the good deeds she does in private, we know that someday God will reward her openly, as it says in Matthew 6:4.

Men from our church helped get the house ready. A painter donated the paint and he and his crew worked all weekend getting the inside done. One landscaper came and replaced all the dead plants with new ones and lined the walk with flowers. Another donates his services to keep the yard looking good on a regular basis. A few days after the house was ready but empty, I went to my monthly community Bible study (BSF) luncheon. This group has women from all different churches in the community studying the Bible together weekly. Once a month we get together for a luncheon and we share what is going on in our lives.

Of course, I was bursting with the news of our house. When it was my turn, I told them that we had been given the use of a house and that we had it all cleaned, painted and ready to go. We just had to furnish it. My small group leader, Nancy, said she had just bought all new leather living room furniture and was thinking about selling her old furniture which was in excellent condition, but that she would be willing to donate it to us. I was thrilled. Little did I know that God was just getting warmed up. Later that day someone from our church called and said, "I heard you got a house for Woman of Gilead. Could you use a desk and chair?" Someone else called and offered some lamps. Someone else a table and chairs. Someone else a sofa. We got pots and pans and end tables and pictures for the wall.

My head was spinning. We were studying Genesis in our Bible study and I immediately thought: this must be what Noah felt like when he saw the animals coming to him, two by two. We had never asked anyone for furniture. It just came, and it came within a 24 hour period! We couldn't have accomplished that if we'd sat down and planned a campaign of soliciting donations. Not only did we get enough furniture to fill each room of the house, but everything matched. Colors and styles seemed like they had been planned. We even had a woman surprise us with an afghan that she had made for us that matched the sofa perfectly.….. without her ever setting foot in the house to see what the furniture looked like!

"…that the God of our Lord Jesus Christ, the Father of glory, may give to you the spirit of wisdom and revelation in the knowledge of Him, the eyes of your understanding being enlightened; that you may know what is the hope of His calling …"

Ephesians 1:16-18

Things I've Learned About God

✝ He Loves Us.

"How priceless is your unfailing love! Both high and low among men find refuge in the shadow of your wings."

Psalm 36:7

I was raised to know that God existed and that Jesus Christ died on the cross for our sins, but it was a very remote idea. He was a remote God, not someone I could actually know. On this journey that began in the bathtub at the lowest point of my life, I have found out that God is not a cold, stern judge who needs to be convinced to love me. God created me lovingly, because He desired to have a close, intimate relationship with me. This relationship, I am finding, is closer than a mother and child. It is more intimate than a husband and wife. It is like no earthly relationship we have ever had or could ever have. There is nothing that I did to earn this, any more than my son had to earn my love the day he was born. I just adored that little bundle. He was mine! My heart nearly burst with love for him. That's how God sees us…but He's God. His love is even more perfect than my love for my son. Hard for me to imagine, but I know it's true. Psalm 139:16-18 says:

"You saw me before I was born.
Every day of my life was recorded in your book.
Every moment was laid out before a single day had passed.

How precious are your thoughts about me, O God.
They cannot be numbered!
I can't even count them; they outnumber the grains of sand!
And when I wake up, you are still with me!"

It's hard to believe, but the God of the Universe thinks about each one of us all the time! Isaiah 49:15 tells us a mother could forget her nursing child before He would forget us. How loved and protected I feel when I read Psalm 17:7-8:

"Show the wonder of your great love,
you who save by your right hand
those who take refuge in you from their foes.

Keep me as the apple of your eye;
hide me in the shadow of your wings"

What safer place can there be than in the shadow of my Father's wings?

✟ He Is Kind.

"For the eyes of the LORD range throughout the earth to strengthen those whose hearts are fully committed to him."

2 Chronicles 16:9

God could have saved me after Pat died. It would still have been the single greatest moment of my life, but He chose to save Pat and me. I think speaks volumes of God's tender kindness. He knew that I would have been haunted by thoughts of Pat not being saved.

From the very beginning He has been so tender to me. I always loved Pat's voice. Not that he was a singer or anything. He couldn't carry a tune with a wheel barrow (neither can I), but I loved his speaking voice. I had meant to record him once I knew he was going to die, but something always came up. Either the camera didn't work or we were out of batteries or we got busy. Something. After he died I had pictures of him, but no sound. I was really sad when I realized I would never hear his voice again. Then one day a couple of months later, I was clearing all the files off my desktop computer to give it away, as I had just about to buy a laptop to bring with me to California. I laboriously went through all 3000+ e-mails to save the few that were important. It had taken about a week. I was rejoicing that I was done, when I suddenly realized I hadn't sifted through the sent mail.

Ugh! Another couple of thousand. These I went through quicker, because I just didn't have the strength to do it as carefully as I had the incoming messages. At the very end I found three emails Pat had sent to our son, David, that I was unaware of. They each had attachments that were voice e-mails that Pat was testing out. The first said "Test". The second said "Hi". The third – oh, the third! – was such a gift. It was a short but sweet message to David that sounded just like Pat, both in the sound and the manner of speech. I cry even as I write this. It meant so much to me and my Father knew it would.

He also knew that Pat's last words on Earth would be very meaningful to me. I had no way of knowing they were his last words at the time, but just before he slipped into a sleep from which he didn't awake, he said one last thing. It wasn't, "I need a drink of water" or "My leg hurts" or anything like that. No, it was the same way he ended each night of our marriage, even by phone on those rare occasions when one of us was out of town. In a very groggy voice and with eyes closed, he whispered, "Good night, Lady. I love you".

When I studied Genesis, we discussed the part where God commands Abraham to sacrifice his son on the altar. I always thought that God was testing Abraham to see if he'd obey, but when we actually thought about it, we realized that God already knew Abraham's heart. He had Abraham go through that ordeal to show Abraham his own heart. About a month or so after that class, I had a dream in which Pat came back. Suddenly he was alive. He was so happy to see me, but I was torn. I still loved him, but I had different life now. He was no longer the center of my world. Jesus was. He saw the look on my face and asked if I was in love with another man. I told him no and he hugged me and said we could deal with anything else.

My heart was breaking, because I was worried that Pat would want to live a different sort of life than I do now. I am no longer interested in the things I used to be interested in, like vacations and shopping. My interests run to Bible study and Prophecy conferences. I now have a life that is 100% available to God. If I had to choose, I would choose God. As much as I loved Pat, I couldn't bear to have my walk with the Lord diminished. Then I woke up and was relieved that I didn't really have to make that choice. Then I realized that God wanted me to know my own heart, that Jesus comes first in my life over everything.

I also had a little incident with a diagnosis that was very telling. I had a routine test done that showed the possibility of something very serious being wrong. I had to refrain from certain foods and drugs like aspirin for 3 days then take a test over a period of 4 days, then turn it in and wait 2 weeks for the results. I told only one person about it because I wanted her to pray with me about it. The thing is, I wasn't worried about it at all – not even when the doctor first told me about it. Death no longer scared me. Of course, a long lingering, painful death would scare me, but not death itself. That was a major change. I used to be terrified of dying. Now that fear is removed. I believe that God had me go through this little trial to show me that I had grown in my faith.

✝ He Takes Care Of Us.

"The LORD is my shepherd; I shall not want."

Psalm 23:1

One of the sweetest things that God has given me is the ability to see His hand in everyday life. When God saved me (and Pat) 3 weeks before Pat's death, I was so excited about my salvation that when He said "Trust Me. Everything will be all right. I will take care of you", I believed Him. I couldn't see how everything could be all right without Pat, but I trusted God. Shortly after the second anniversary of Pat's death, I suddenly noticed that many of the people around me have some major trait of Pat's!

My friend Kim Newton has the faith to believe in the impossible just like Pat did. I am so down-to-Earth that I would have missed out on so much if Pat hadn't been there to lift my sights. My other friend, Kim Paden, is a prolific idea person. If you asked Pat for an idea for some particular thing, he gave you 500 ideas. You had to beg him to stop. Kim has that same creative streak. My friend Laura has been my supporter and encourager since I first arrived in town. Just like Pat, she always tells me I can do things that I don't think I can. My friend Eliot is the liaison between Women of Gilead and the church. She checks to see that we have what we need, but she always keeps an eye on me personally. She wants to know that I am getting enough rest, that I am not getting burned out, that I have someone to unburden myself to. I have a tendency to be everyone's mother. With Pat, I always knew someone in the world was looking out for me.

My friend Jeanne "gets" me. I don't have to explain much. She just understands me. Pat always "got" me. I loved that. My son, Mike, was born 40 years old. I have listened to and been impressed by his opinions since he was a child. It is so comforting to know that, if I have to make an important decision, he is there to give me sound advice, just like Pat. Last but not least, my son David (who lives with me) and I laugh so much. We get downright silly. He sometimes has to crawl out of the room so he can breathe. Pat and I used to laugh a lot. We often said it was the key to the success of our marriage.

So God kept His promise. He did make everything all right. He lovingly set about creating a life for me that would include all that I need and He allowed me to realize it!

✝ He Has A Sense Of Humor.

One morning I got a call from a friend who needed a ride to Western Union to wire money to a relative. I left the house in a bit of a hurry because I wanted to get her there and then get on to Gilead House. On the way there I realized I hadn't brushed my teeth. For over 50 years, I never left the house without brushing my teeth. I couldn't figure out what was up with that. Fortunately Western Union is at a drug store so I thought I'd just pick up a tube of toothpaste and a travel toothbrush to leave at Gilead in case I ever do that again. Since the travel toothbrushes came in a set of two, I had an extra.

I got to Gilead, brushed my teeth, and then the phone rang. I was there holding the extra toothbrush and toothpaste in my left hand and the phone in my right hand. The call was from a woman in a lockdown psychiatric facility who was in desperate need of someone to come pray with her. She was also in desperate need of a toothbrush and some toothpaste. It took about 5 seconds to raise my eyes and say "Oh… I get it!" I could almost see God grinning down at me. I love that! It may seem like such a small thing, but it means that the Creator of the universe decided to use me to help this woman. It didn't matter how He used me. It matters that He did. This kind of intimate contact makes me feel complete. It makes me feel loved. It makes me love Him more.

✝ He Provides For Us.

"On the mountain of the LORD it will be provided."

Genesis 22:14

We'd had a yard sale to raise some funds to help us get Women of Gilead started. A couple of us committed a certain amount each month to keep it going, but we were about $300 short of our estimated monthly expenses. Our rent was very, very low, but we still had utilities, phone, Internet and miscellaneous operating expenses. Although I was not in the habit of worrying about how Women of Gilead would come together, since God had so obviously been orchestrating everything down to the minutest detail, I did start to worry about this monthly shortfall. I prayed about it and then put it in the back of my mind. Later that day, a friend called and told me she wanted to support this ministry and she was going to send us $300 per month! When you see God provide so consistently and so precisely, how can you ever doubt His love and concern for us? Or His sovereignty?

✝ He Is Sovereign.

"How great are your works, O LORD, how profound your thoughts!"

Psalm 92:5

While I was on a trip to Israel, I sat at breakfast with my friend Laura. We were just chatting and a girl from our group went by. Laura mentioned that the girl used to cut herself, had been delivered of it and now worked with young girls who do that to try to help them through prayer and support.

A few days later we went back home. The next day, I went to Gilead to pick up my cell phone. Kim Paden was covering for me and we got talking about my trip and things that had happened at Gilead while I was gone. I only meant to stay a few minutes, but I ended up staying for over an hour. Then a woman stopped in with her 20-year-old niece whom she said needed prayer. The niece was very quiet. We talked a little bit to introduce ourselves, but the niece remained quiet. Finally I moved to a spot right in front of the niece and looked her in the eye. I asked her why she needed prayer. She very quietly and hesitatingly said that she was in a bad relationship and she didn't take good care of herself. When someone says to me that they don't take good care of themselves, I usually interpret that to mean they don't eat right, don't exercise, don't take vitamins, etc.

Without thinking, I said, "Do you hurt yourself?" I shocked myself by saying that, but tears began rolling down her cheeks and she said, "I cut myself". I was able to connect her with the girl from my Israel trip. I couldn't have done that unless the One who is sovereign over all things had arranged for my divine appointments. I just happened to be having breakfast with Laura at the time that girl walked by. She just happened to tell me about her group. A few days later I happened to stop in Gilead on the very day that the woman and her niece came in and I just happened to delay long enough to be there when they did. Those things didn't just happen. They were arranged. Before I knew who God really was, I gave a lot of credence to coincidences. Not any more. I'm a believer!

✟ He Is The One Who Saves.

"The Lord is not slow in keeping his promise, as some understand slowness. He is patient with you, not wanting anyone to perish, but everyone to come to repentance."

I recently had a family member from back in New York come out for a visit with her family. I had not seen any of them since I left New York. They were passing through Santa Barbara and I was only going to have an afternoon with her. That evening we would join the rest of the family and my two sons for a dinner out. So I figured I had about three hours to tell her everything she needed to know for eternal life. The plan was to pick her up and show her around Santa Barbara. As I prayed, I asked God how I was going to be able to witness to her in such a short time. She was a lapsed Catholic. She didn't know the Bible. She didn't know how to have a relationship with Jesus. She didn't know that you don't pray to Mary or to saints or to anyone other than God. She was where I was 2½ years prior.

I knew exactly how much she didn't know and it overwhelmed me. I began to give in to frustration. How could I know what to leave out and what to include and how to do it in such a way that she would hear it? It would all be new to her and I only had a few hours. I was deeply distressed. It was just impossible. Then I remembered God's track record. I prayed, "Lord, You are the God of impossibilities. You can do all things. Go before me. Prepare her heart. I don't know how to do this, but You do." I think the Lord got a good laugh over this one. I picked her up and started showing her State Street and all the shops. She said that was nice, but then she asked me a Bible question. I gave her a nice thorough answer and then I showed her Stearns Wharf.

Again, she said, very nice, but wanted to know about salvation. It took me a few minutes to realize: here I am showing her tourist sights when what she wants to know about is faith and salvation. Can you hear the giggling from above? We got a couple of iced teas and sat down to talk. We covered a wide range of topics and at the end of the afternoon, she made a profession of faith. I had prayed that I could find a way for me to tell her about Him, and what He did was get her to do the asking. I told her about the church I went to for 2 months before I moved to

California, the one where I was baptized and gave my testimony for the first time.

It turns out the church is only a mile from her house, she had recently checked out the associated Christian school for her son, and her friend had asked her to go there with her! She is a school teacher and the type of person who does not give up. She is sweet, gentle and lovable, but extremely tenacious. Perfect to go back and tell the good news to her brothers, sisters and cousins.

✠ He Is Holy.

"…you were sealed with the Holy Spirit of promise, who is the guarantee of our inheritance until the redemption of the purchased possession, to the praise of His glory."

Ephesians 1:13-14

When we are saved, we receive the Holy Spirit inside of us. He is there to guide us and teach us and empower us to live beyond ourselves. We are able to better know God's will. We are sensitized to good and evil. God is holy. He cannot abide sin. When we are filled with His Holy Spirit, we also find sin repugnant. I experienced what I think of as a tiny sample of what God experiences when He beholds sin. I went to a movie for the first time in awhile. You have to realize that I got rid of my TV because of all the junk on it. I only hang out with Christians and I only read Christian books. My full-time "job" is praying and talking to people about God. I pretty much live in a Christian bubble. This is not because I have to, it is because I want to. This is what brings me joy and satisfaction.

So, this movie seemed harmless enough to me at first, but it began to get more and more off-color. Eventually it was making me ill. I couldn't leave, because I was in the center of the row and I am completely blinded in the dark. I was so horrified at the images on the screen that I spent the last third of the movie with my eyes closed. I got home and cried my eyes out. I felt so dirty. I couldn't handle something that probably wouldn't have fazed me at all a few years ago. I read my Bible for a couple of hours to try to cleanse my mind of the filth I had allowed to enter it. If one movie which wasn't considered that bad by most people, could make me feel actually sick, how must God feel when He sees our sin?

✝ He Always Blesses Obedience.

"And my God shall supply all your need according to His riches in glory by Christ Jesus."

Philippians 4:19

I made a decision to obey God to the best of my ability. Every time I do something that brings me out of my comfort zone, even sometimes outright scaring me, He gets me through it and then blesses me for it. Even though I live on a tight budget, I have spent money I couldn't afford to do something that I believe God was asking me to do. Each time, He replaces the money in some unexpected way. Each time my faith and trust grow stronger and stronger.

In my old life, I would have looked at my meager income and the cost of living in Santa Barbara and I would have cut way down on money given to the church or to charity. I now believe what God says in Malachi 3:10 regarding tithes. It's the only place in the Bible that God challenges us to test Him. He says if we give Him His due, He will pour an abundance of blessings on us. The way my needs get met with the resources I have just doesn't make sense unless you factor in God.

✝ He Protects Us.

"You are my hiding place; you will protect me from trouble and surround me with songs of deliverance."

Psalm 32:7

I believe that God sometimes protects His people from themselves and from the world long before they ever accept Him into their hearts. I truly believe He did that in my life. I was 54 years old when I accepted Jesus as my Lord and Savior, but I can look back at my life and see Him at work in my childhood and teenage years, as well as my adult life. I made some very poor choices (and, I might add, dangerous ones) when I was in high school and college. I drank too much, not because I had an addiction, but because it was what we did. We drank and danced and allowed people we didn't know to give us rides home. I even hitchhiked alone once when I had been drinking.

So many times I could have become a statistic. I was a naïve girl raised in rural upstate New York. I never even heard a swear word until I was 16 years old. I was very protected, but at age seventeen I found myself at college in a large city with virtually no supervision. I know my parents loved me, but they thought the best they could do for me was shield me from the gritty side of the world. They never taught me anything about the facts of life or about anything I should know to keep myself safe. So basically I was a blinking target waiting for any predator to come along and ravish me.

But that is not what my Father in heaven had for me! Even though I was very young and ignorant, my Father protected me in every situation. I know that someday I am going to come face to face with one frazzled-looking guardian angel and I am going to give him a big old hug of thanks!

Here's just one example of what I am talking about: a week after I got to school, there was a beer blast at a university that was about 45 minutes away from my college. I rode up there with some upper class girls from my dorm (I really didn't know them yet) and we danced and guzzled some beer, and then they decided to go to a party at someone's apartment. I went along and after a little while, I looked around and they had gone. To make matters worse, a drunken student wouldn't leave me alone.

So here I was, 17 years old, in an apartment filled with strangers, many of whom were drunk. I didn't know the telephone number at my dorm and wouldn't know who could come get me even if I could tell them where I was! I had no money on me. I was a little nervous. Then this nice guy from that university offered to drive me home. With relief, I accepted. On the way home, he pulled over in a lover's lane type area and tried to convince me to get into the back seat with him. I kept resisting him and he finally said he wouldn't drive me home if I didn't.

Without thinking, I said, "If you had a sister my age, would you think it was alright for her to do that?" He winced and his shoulders slumped. After a short silence, he told me he did have a sister my age. She even went to my school. And no, he wouldn't want that for her. He turned the motor back on and drove me home. For the rest of that year (he was a senior, I was a freshman) he was like a big brother to me, always looking across the room at school events, checking out who I was dancing with, shooing away any who were "bad news". I truly believe that the Holy Spirit put those words in my mouth, the very words that would have the most impact on him.

✝ He Wants Our Best.

"I can do all things through Christ who strengthens me."

Philippians 4:13

I used to be very shy. I would totally freeze up in the presence of more than 2 people. The idea of actually getting up in front of people to speak would terrify me. In high school, I used to take a zero, rather than stand up and read my homework. I would lie and say I hadn't done it. That is so sad. I was convinced that people would laugh at me, because anything I had to say would be stupid. I was also convinced that I was ugly. I had friends and always had a boyfriend, but still my self-image was pretty bad. Pat helped me get over a lot of that by his consistent love and encouragement. He always believed in me. That was something I never experienced before.

When I turned my life over to God for His use, I said I would do anything He asked of me. Much to my dismay, at times that has included getting up in front of a room full or church full of people to speak. The first time was at my baptism. I stood on a stage with five other people in front of an audience of what seemed like thousands of people – it was probably more like 300. I had to give my testimony for the very first time. I wrote it out very carefully and read it over and over. I expected to read it, but was worried I wouldn't be able to see the print from the podium. I worried a lot about this over the 2 months that I was preparing for it. I looked up every scripture I could on fear. My favorite was Isaiah 41:10

"Fear not, for I am with you; Be not dismayed, for I am your God. I will strengthen you, Yes, I will help you, I will uphold you with My righteous right hand."

I prayed about it and sometimes I was a little calmer than other times.

On the day of the baptism I was terrified, but obediently I walked up to the podium as though I were walking to my execution. I opened my mouth and hoped something would come out. Then for the first time I consciously experienced the Holy Spirit enabling me to do something I couldn't have done on my own. Even though I fully expected to stutter and stammer and embarrass myself, the Holy Spirit allowed me to speak naturally, coherently and without ever looking at my written speech. I was totally stunned. Since I was last to speak, we all walked off the stage and, once behind the curtain, my legs were so rubbery, I had to lean against the wall to keep from falling down. I couldn't believe what God had just done. Many times since I have remembered what He did that day, and it has given me the courage to do something He has asked that seemed impossible for me.

As I said before, public speaking is not on my list of fun things to do, but if the Lord asks... Not long ago, Reality, the church in Carpinteria that I also attend, asked me to give my testimony at their Women's Worship night. I was, as usual, fearful of getting up there, but I said "Yes". The worst part was that I had to pare down my testimony to 10 minutes. When I practiced it a couple of times, it was closer to 20 minutes, and that was by condensing and leaving a lot out. I really struggled more with the time issue than the public speaking part. Finally I got it close enough, but I didn't want to read it, because I wanted the Holy Spirit to guide me. So I prayed for two things: that I would honor the time restriction the church had requested, and that the Spirit would guide me to include what that particular audience needed to hear and leave out anything they didn't.

The night before the event, I was rushing to get out the door to teach a Bible study at Women's Real Life at Calvary Chapel. I carried a big pot of boiling water across the kitchen to the sink. The pot spilled the scalding water all over my legs and feet. I waited for the pain, but it didn't come. I set the pot down and looked at my legs. They were wet. My feet were drenched and my sandals were squishing with water, and yet they were not burned. They weren't even red. In fact, I felt no heat at all. I tested my legs, thinking I might have lost feeling due to the MS, but they were normal.

I cautiously dipped my finger in the remaining water in the pot and it was, in fact, extremely hot. I was completely confused, but I just accepted that God had miraculously protected me. The next evening, when I got to the Reality, I found that everyone involved with the Worship Night had been under some form of spiritual attack. The singers had even lost their voices. I realized then that the enemy had tried to stop us, but God wouldn't let him. I love being on the winning side! That night God answered my prayers. The Holy Spirit spoke through me and everything went well. I actually enjoyed it. Me, speaking in public, enjoying it. Unbelievable, but true. Several women came up to me to tell me that something I had shared really touched them.

I was so filled with gratitude for what God done...again. I had grown up not feeling acceptable. God was showing me that in His family, I am accepted and I am loved. I am finding that the thrill I feel when I am speaking about God and His goodness is stronger than the fear of speaking in public. I have stopped saying "I am not..." or "I can not...". I am who God says I am and I can do whatever He says I can do. This is a truth that sounded good to me, but I didn't embrace at first. Now, after seeing what He will do in my life, if I let Him be in charge, I am exhilarated by the possibilities!

In fact, during the time I was preparing for this event and trying to figure out what to cut, I prayed and I mentioned to God that there was so much He had done in my life in these past 2 ½ years that I didn't know how to trim it. That was when the idea of a book first entered my mind. I had never entertained the idea of writing anything. I wasn't sure if God was asking me to write a book or if it was my own idea. I asked Him to send me confirmation. I didn't want to devote the time and effort required to write a book if it wasn't His idea. I told no one that I was thinking about it.

At the Women's Worship night, an acquaintance came up and told me I should write a book. When she saw the look on my face, she said, "That's confirmation, huh?" I nodded. Whoa, I was going to write a book! That both scared and excited me. My natural reaction is "I'm not a writer!", but I have given up all decisions to the Lord, so whatever He decides is what is going to happen. On the drive home, however, I thought that maybe this was just a coincidence. After all, I had just told the group some stories of what God had done and intimated that there was a lot more that I could tell them. Maybe she would just naturally say something like that.

So that night in prayer I asked God to send me a second confirmation. I wanted to make sure I was doing what He wanted. I sort of felt like Gideon with his fleece asking God to confirm twice, but since He seemed OK with Gideon doing it, I figured He wouldn't mind me following his example. After all, all scripture is written for our instruction. I asked the Lord to have someone come up to me and say the exact words, "Carol, you need to write a book". I didn't want to get carried away interpreting different statements to mean what I wanted them to mean. I also asked that it would be within the week. I didn't want to have it constantly on my mind, distracting me from everything else. Exactly one week to the day later, a friend said, "Carol, you need to write a book". There it was.

✟ He Is Our Peace.

"He got up, rebuked the wind and said to the waves, "Quiet! Be still!" Then the wind died down and it was completely calm."

Mark 4:39

The world teaches us that, if only we had this and this and this, then we'd be happy. And it's true. For a little while we are happy with what we have, but it doesn't last. Only the soul-satisfying peace that comes from being in fellowship God can fill the emptiness inside. Jesus said in John 10:10,

"The thief does not come except to steal, and to kill, and to destroy. I have come that they may have life, and that they may have it more abundantly."

Many of us think if only we had the right spouse, or if only we had children, or if only we could lose enough weight, or if only we had enough money, we'd be satisfied. That kind of happiness is fleeting. There is always more to be had. The thief Jesus refers to is the enemy of our soul, Satan, who loves to keep us longing for things so that we are not longing for God. In the process, we have no peace. We need more things and more thrills to satisfy us. Focusing on Jesus brings us peace, because when we put our faith in Him, He can calm the storms in our lives. Casting our cares on Him takes them off our shoulders. He is unchanging. He is the Rock. Only He can fill that empty place inside us.

✝ We Need Him.

"Satisfy us in the morning with your unfailing love, that we may sing for joy and be glad all our days."

Psalm 90:14

I never used to think about God unless there was a serious problem in my life. Even then, He was the last resort. I exhausted all other avenues of relief first. I have learned to come to God first and sometimes only to Him, but more than that, I have begun to spend time with Him each morning just enjoying His presence, remembering what He did in order to bring me into fellowship with Him, praising His holiness and His goodness. It seems on the surface that this is all for His benefit, but what happens is that I am changed. My joy is heightened. I am strengthened. I am the one who benefits! Funny how that works. Only God could come up with something that unique.

Reading this account of my life, you may think I pretty much turned from the loss of my husband and never looked back. To some extent that is true. I have been so blessed as to be given a new and exciting second life, but I do miss Pat. Every day. I talk about him all the time with my sons and with my friends. There are sweet memories and some funny stories of our life together. There are, however, moments when I really feel a pang about Pat not being here. There have been times when I have left church with my heart just bursting with excitement over something I just learned. I have thought to myself, "I can't wait to get home and tell Pat!" only to remember sadly that Pat isn't there. In my heart I know without a doubt that Pat is with the Lord and he is perfectly happy. That makes me happy, but I do still miss him.

I'll see a couple walk by who remind me of Pat and me. They're holding hands. The guy has on cargo shorts with all the pockets. They're laughing over some shared secret. I'll feel my heart start to ache and my eyes fill with tears. I give myself a minute to feel the feelings. Just one minute, then I combat the sadness with the Truth. I begin praying and listing all the things that I have been given: eternal life, the chance to know my God in such an intimate way, the promise that I will see Him in person one day, along with Pat. I have been given an opportunity to participate in Kingdom work on the front lines. I have been given a joy that is founded on the solid foundation of Jesus Christ, independent of any circumstances in my life. I lost much, but I have been given so much more. When you fix your eyes on Jesus, you cannot continue to feel sorry for yourself. It just can't happen.

Recently at a home group, we were each asked to come the first evening prepared to tell what we are passionate about and bring something that represents that. The example given was someone who loves music might bring a guitar pick. I really struggled with this for days. Other than the Lord and my two sons (both pretty obvious answers) I could not think of a single thing I was passionate about. I used to love programming. I could get "lost" in the process of making a computer program do what I wanted it to do and do it with style. I used to read at least one mystery novel a week. I used to love to go shopping. It didn't matter if it was for clothes or groceries or hardware items. I just plain loved shopping. Travel was a huge passion of mine. Pat and I used to go on really terrific vacations: biking through France, a romantic trip through Italy, hangliding in Kitty Hawk, sailing in the San Juan Islands. I used to really like lots of things. Now they all seem so meaningless. I don't want to spend significant amounts of time on something that doesn't have to do with Jesus Christ. He is my passion. It might sound corny, but it is true.

I was not brought up in a household in which the Bible was read or discussed. We went to church, but it was really just an obligation. We were happy when some reason came up like a huge snowstorm or car trouble that meant we didn't have to go to church. What a difference it makes to truly have God in your life! Now I look forward to church. It is exciting to me. I have been doubly blessed to have not just one great church, but two. Calvary Chapel Santa Barbara and Reality Carpinteria are both dynamic, truth-telling, Bible-based evangelical churches that have nurtured my passion to know God. The pastoral staffs at both churches, led by Ricky Ryan and Britt Merrick, are Spirit-led servants who take their calling seriously. God has anointed these men to speak His truth with integrity and with passion. My life has been influenced immensely by their teaching.

As a result of my upbringing, I was not taught how to have a relationship with Jesus Christ. I didn't know how to pray (other than memorized prayers). I didn't even know that I needed saving. I had never heard the term used in that context before. I thought if you knew who Jesus Christ was, that was enough. I didn't know the Bible. In fact, I didn't even know if all of the Bible was true. I didn't know how to discern God's will. After I was saved, a trait I have always thought of as a weakness in me became a strength. In 1 Corinthians 1:27-28 it says that God chooses the foolish things of the world to confound the wise.

I have always been a bit naïve and trusting. People who were skeptical about everything always seemed wiser than me. However, in God's economy, my willingness to trust Him in spite of not knowing every detail, trusting Him to show me whatever I needed to know, wasn't treated as foolishness. He has tenderly taught me things and gently corrected me. He has protected me from harm and from being shamed. He is the perfect Father. The One who really can look out for His child and protect her. Earthly fathers may try, but He can do it.

When I was still learning how to pray, I was told that there was an acronym that was helpful: A.C.T.S. which stood for Adoration (praise), Confession, Thanksgiving and Supplication (asking). I knew how to confess and how to thank God and there isn't anyone I know who doesn't instinctively know how to ask for things, but I was really stumped by the adoration. I didn't know what to say to praise Him. So I prayed that He would teach me. I heard someone on the radio who said you should say "I praise you, Lord" ten times, but that just didn't seem right to me. It seemed lazy, like it wasn't worth the effort of figuring out what to specifically praise Him for. So I prayed for Him to teach me for a couple of weeks. Then one morning I thought, "I know, I'll just list who He is and what He has done".

That opened up such a floodgate of prayer and praise that I wound up being an hour and a half late for work. I was tempted to mark on my time slip that the reason I was late was that I couldn't stop praising the Lord, but I chickened out! I started out saying things like, "You are the God that created all things. You created the stars and the sun and the moon and mountains and the ocean. You invented color and music and laughter and butterflies. You made thousands of different types of trees. Tall evergreens and palm trees and maple trees and cactus and flowers like tulips and roses and violets and lilies. You made whales and elephants and dogs and cats and lions...." My list went on and on and as I just kept speaking the things that He spoke into existence, my heart began to fill with praise and thanksgiving and love for Him. I wanted to talk to Him forever. It's no wonder that I lost interest in my job. It took me away from the Love of my life.

✝ He Is Gracious

"The LORD is gracious and righteous; our God is full of compassion."

Psalm 116:5

I believe that Pat and I were given an "advance" blessing in our marriage. I know that God made Pat for me and me for Pat. We were so suited to each other and helped to heal each other from hurts from our childhoods, but I am referring to the type of marriage that is described in the Bible. Neither of us was familiar with the Bible at all. We probably could have named maybe 5 of the 66 books by name, yet we had a pretty biblically sound marriage. I submitted to Pat's authority as head of our family, but never felt inferior to him. He was generous and encouraging and protective of me and I of him. We put each other's interests first. I was always stunned by young women who insisted on their rights and independence from the start. They were determined to make their man do their bidding.

Of course, these marriages always turned out to be disasters. They were focused on self. Even though Pat and I did not know Jesus as Lord of our lives, we were blessed with an innate sense of how a marriage should be conducted. We extended each other grace, though we weren't familiar with the word or its meaning. When we argued, we never said things that were designed to hurt. Therefore, making up was so much easier. I've often heard someone describe an argument with their spouse and things were said that couldn't be unsaid. Even though they had technically made up, the hurt lingered. We didn't sit down and decide how we would fight, but it evolved. I know that was the Holy Spirit. All good things come from above.

We had a rule in our house that got quite a workout when our sons were teenagers. You weren't allowed to go to bed angry (Sound familiar? Ephesians 4:26) and you couldn't just apologize. You had to restore fellowship. My husband sometimes lost his temper when one of our sons forgot to do something he was told to do over and over. After a 9-hour hectic work day and 2-hour commute, he would just lose it and mete out some overly harsh penalty. Later on when he cooled off, he would say to me, "I guess I was too hard on David. I shouldn't have gotten that mad." I always said, "Don't tell me. Tell him." Pat would walk down the hall. I would hear a muffled conversation and then giggling. Soon they were wrestling and laughing and all would be back to normal.

I have to tell you, this very principle is one of the reasons we were able to deal with Pat's unexpected death as well as we did. There were no scars or unresolved issues between any of us. Everyone in our family felt loved by the rest. Our relationships received continual nurturing. That isn't something we could have accomplished on our own. Left to our own devices, we would have been more focused on self, but God blessed us with an "advance". He knew we were going to love Him and I think He just wanted to bless us. He didn't owe us anything, but He is generous and kind and blesses whom He chooses to bless.

I believe that my marriage to Pat was a foretaste of my relationship with Jesus. Of course, my marriage was not perfect, but it did show me great love and self-sacrifice. It showed me the importance of the little things. There are husbands who routinely make grand gestures to their wives, but are severely lacking in the small, day-to-day interactions that are the strength of a relationship. Pat sometimes did the grand gesture, but he was an expert in showing his love by wanting to spend lots of time with me, by wanting to share every little thing that happened during the day, by the look in his eyes every time he saw me, by the way he spoke about me to other people when I wasn't around. Long after I wasn't so young or so cute anymore, he still seemed to see me that way. His love and fidelity was something I never had occasion to question.

I have found that my relationship with Jesus follows a similar pattern. He did do the big things for me: He became a man and came to Earth to live a perfect life; He suffered and died a horrible death for me on the cross; He willingly took on unimaginable sorrow for my sake; but every day, in a million smaller ways, He shows me He loves me. He answers my prayers. He lets me see something beautiful in a scripture that I had not seen before. He will suddenly "turn the light on" when I'm reading something I have read many times. He will guide me out of harm's way. He urges me to keep silent about something I would have blurted out, only to find out later that it would have been messy, had I spoken.

He corrects me in sweet, gentle ways. He has taught me to come to Him immediately in prayer, then He guides me to an appropriate scripture when something upsetting happens. He has taught me to forgive quickly and generously. He has put loving people in my life who uplift me. He has forgiven me every time I mess up. I never have to wallow in guilt. He allows me to hear a scripture or a teaching at the exact moment I need to hear it. He fills my heart with excitement over little things that I know are from Him. He makes a way where there is no way. He gives me peace of mind over things that I cannot change. He fills my life with good things. He has made me content with what I have and I have no desire for what I don't have. He is the joy of my life!

Conclusion

I'm an ordinary person. There is nothing extraordinary about me. It is the One I worship who is extraordinary. God certainly didn't call me to write this book because I am a great writer. I'm not. He didn't call me to teach because I am a great scholar. Again, I'm not. God has chosen to use me for His purposes and I have been so blessed by it. It's like an old wooden ladle that is used to scoop up melted gold. What happens to the ladle? It gets coated with gold. It becomes something special, not because it is inherently valuable, but because it has been dipped in the gold. That is what it is like to be used by God. When He uses you to bless someone, you also receive a blessing.

I guess if there is one thing I would like to leave you with, it is this: you don't have to have it all figured out. I know I don't. Trust God completely. Know that He will never let you down. He will never turn against you. The world teaches us to keep our guard up, to never completely let it down for anyone. You might get hurt. It is different with the Lord. The more you expose your heart to Him, the more He can do in your life. The more you allow yourself to be vulnerable before Him, the more you will be blessed. He loves you passionately. He always has and He always will.

Jeremiah 29:11 says He has plans for you, plans for good and not for disaster. Plans to give you a future and a hope. This is a promise that God made to the nation of Israel, but it expresses His heart toward all of us who love Him. Trust Him. Let Him bless your life. Let Him show you the eternal blessing He has in store for you.

As a computer programmer, I had to boil things down to a simple but accurate flow of logic. So here is the logic I came up with concerning Jesus:

+ In our heart of hearts, we know there is a God. He has put an inner knowledge of His existence in each of us, though many will deny Him, because they don't want to humble themselves to anyone, not even God. By denying His existence they can live any way they want to. They don't have to answer to Him.

+ So if you can admit there is a God, then it makes sense to find out what He expects from us so we don't have any huge surprises after we die (no one denies that we will all die).

+ He left us a manual. We ought to read it. Too often, we develop an opinion about the Bible without ever studying it. I know because that's what I did and, to my shame, exemplified to my children. They now have to bear the price of my negligence. Some of the untruths that I bought into without ever checking it out: "the Old Testament and the New Testament totally conflict with each other", "God was violent and judgmental in the Old Testament but loving and kind in the New Testament, therefore He changed", "some of those stories are just made up as lessons to us", and "the Bible has lots of inconsistencies". I didn't get it, but neither did I ever study it. Once you begin to study the Bible, it no longer seems laborious. It is beautiful and comforting and instructive. It doesn't leave you feeling condemned and hopeless. It shows you the right way and gives you strength and peace of mind. It shows that God never changes. That is true freedom.

+ The Bible says Jesus is the Way, the Truth, and the Life. He is the truth of God. Look at Jesus' life and you will see God. Listen to His words and you will hear God. He is the way. "No one comes to the Father except through Me." If there had been any other way for us to be saved, God would not have sent His only Son to die on the cross. Why would He?

If you have never accepted Jesus Christ as Lord of your life, don't put it off. Do it now. It's not hard. It's very simple. We tend to make things way more complicated than they need to be. All you have to do is admit you cannot live a blameless life on your own. You are a sinner and you need a Savior. God came to earth in order to reach out to us. He draped Himself in humanity as the man, Jesus Christ, and He paid for all our sins. He offers us an eternity of bliss if we will accept His free gift. If we don't accept Him as Lord, if we do not allow Him to "drive", we will miss out on the greatest prize of all time. Do not be fooled into thinking that, if you are a good person, you will get into heaven because, after all, God is loving and forgiving, isn't He? Yes, He is, but He is also holy. He is just and fair. He will not turn a blind eye to sin. He is merciful and compassionate, but He will not wait forever. All sin will be judged and paid for.

It's up to you whether you want to pay for it yourself or you want to accept Jesus' gift. God's Word tells us that Jesus is the only way to get to heaven. In today's politically correct society, this is not a popular position. It is considered harsh and biased. The concept of absolute truth is not comfortable. We would rather accept truth that fits our comfort level. The problem is, we didn't create the universe and we don't get to make the rules. You may not like gravity, but you will fall if you jump off a building. It doesn't matter if it seems harsh and unfair to you. It is the truth. It is like a drowning person who resists the one who attempts to save him, when it would all be so much easier and safer if he would just go limp and let the rescuer do his job. It would be for our benefit if we would only stop fighting God and submit to Him and let Him rescue us.

Absolute truth is unchanging. It is solid. If we base our "truth" on what is acceptable to most people, it will be continually changing as people change. Eventually we would become a lawless, chaotic society where everyone is out for themselves. It is only when we place our trust in our unchanging God that we will have stability, safety and decency.

If you want to ask Jesus to be your Lord and Savior, it is as simple as asking Him to do just that. There are no special words you need to say. There is no exact formula prayer, but here is a sample: "Jesus, I know that

I am a sinner and that I deserve to pay for my sins. However, I am asking you to be my personal Lord and Savior and to take control of my life. I believe that your death and resurrection paid my debt. Thank you Lord, for saving me and forgiving me! Amen!"

Believe Him. Trust Him. You can't even imagine what He has in store for you if you do!

"No eye has seen, no ear has heard, no mind has conceived what God has prepared for those who love him"

Appendix

Carol Smullens
   Email: carol@smullens.com

Calvary Chapel Santa Barbara
   1 N. Calle Cesar Chavez, Suite 21
   Santa Barbara, CA 93103
   Phone: 805.730.1400
   Email: info@calvarychapelsb.com
   Website: www.calvarychapelsb.com

Reality Carpinteria
   5251 Sixth Street
   Carpinteria, CA 93013
   Phone: 805.684.5247
   Email: office@realitycarp.com
   Website: www.jesusisreality.com

Women of Gilead
A Ministry of Calvary Chapel Santa Barbara
   Email: womenofgilead@yahoo.com
   Website: www.womenofgilead.com

Women's Real Life
A Ministry of Calvary Chapel Santa Barbara
   Email: carol@womensrl.com
   Website: www.womensrl.com

Loudonville Community Church

374 Loudon Road
Loudonville, NY 12211
Phone: 518.436.9601
Email: lcc@lcchurch.org
Website: www.lcchurch.org

R.O.C.K Ministries
Website: www.rockministries.org

"Romans Road" is a series of verses from the Bible, in the book of Romans, that map out the path to salvation. It explains our condition without God, His grace and mercy toward us, and what our response to Him ought to be in light of what He has done.

Romans 3:23 "For all have sinned, and come short of the glory of God." We have all sinned. We have all done things that are displeasing to God. There is no one who is innocent. Jesus is the only person who ever lived a pure and sinless life.

Romans 6:23 "For the wages of sin is death; but the gift of God is eternal life through Jesus Christ our Lord." The punishment that we have earned for our sins is death. Not just physical death, but eternal death!

Romans 5:8 "But God demonstrates His own love toward us, in that while we were still sinners, Christ died for us." Jesus' death on the cross paid the price of our sins. Jesus' resurrection proves that God accepted Jesus' death as the payment for our sins.

Romans 10:9 "if you confess with your mouth Jesus as Lord, and believe in your heart that God raised Him from the dead, you will be saved." Jesus died to pay the penalty for our sins and to rescue us from eternal death. Salvation is available to anyone who chooses to trust in Jesus Christ as their Lord and Savior.

Romans 5:1 "Therefore, since we have been justified through faith, we have peace with God through our Lord Jesus Christ." Through Jesus Christ we have fellowship with God. Romans 8:1 tells us, "Therefore, there is now no condemnation for those who are in Christ Jesus." Because of Jesus' death on our behalf, we will never be condemned for our sins. Romans 8:38-39 further promises that no one and nothing in all creation can separate us from the love of God that is in Christ Jesus.